Shambhala Warriors

Warriors

Nonviolent fighters for peace

By Teddy Milne

PITTENBRUACH PRESS   NORTHAMPTON, MA

D0851017

Copyright © 1987 by Teddy Milne
All rights reserved.
Shambala illustration by James A. Milne
Library of Congress Catalog No. 86-64054
ISBN 0-938875-07-8

First Printing 1987   Printed in USA
10 9 8 7 6 5 4 3 2

Published by
PITTENBRUACH PRESS, 15 Walnut St., PO Box 553
                    Northampton, MA 01061

Other books by Teddy Milne: (see coupon at end
        of this book)
    Peace Porridge One: Kids as Peacemakers
    Peace Porridge Two: Russia to Begin With
    War is a Dinosaur, and other songs of hope,
        love and weltschmerz
    Choose Love
    Anthony
    Be Your Own Boss (Great Britain only)

CONTENTS

The story

The course

The songs

CHAPTER ONE: Callifree
****

Callifree panted on up to the sunny rock that
jutted out above her. That would be a good place
to rest and look around.

She had never been up in the hills before,
and hadn't realized how tiring it was to make her
way up through the bushes that grabbed at you as
you passed.

She got to the top of the rock and crept out
gingerly, looking around her. Her eyes lit up
with astonishment as she saw her village down in
the valley for the first time from above, with
its trim huts and neat gardens. That tiny figure
in black must be Auntie Timten, and perhaps that
speck running across the field was little Istobel,
Halred's sister. Callifree eagerly identified her
own house, and then others, looking like children's toys far below.

A cloud covered the sun for an instant, and
she shivered as the cool breeze swept across her
sweating back. Fearfully, her eyes followed the
fields across the valley toward South Mountain,

and then up across the dark forest and the hummocky hills to where the smoke from the hill village curled up to the peaks.

She studied the forest carefully, looking for any sign of movement, but there was none. Then she rolled over, searching upward for the tiny wisp of smoke that hung above her destination. Yes, there it was, she had been heading straight for it, despite the lack of any path. Pleased with herself, she searched the way that lay between, looking for any difficulties, but it looked easy enough, though steep.

Another cloud passed, and Callifree bit her lip. The heat that had sent her running toward the Witch of West Mountain had long since gone in the heat of the climb. Perhaps she should think it over again.

It was her cousin Torko that had set her off. In his sneering way he had called her a sissy girl, afraid of her own shadow, and not like the tough valley men who went off to war regularly. For as long as she could remember, her village had been at war with the hill village above, and her own parents had been killed several years ago, along with many other villagers.

She had been trying to talk with Torko, asking why it wouldn't be better to stop warring and be at peace, and he had laughed at her. "Go off to the Witch if you want peace," he had sneered. "They say she's as cowardly as you are."

Callifree knew that the hill people called her Bethaa the Wise, and didn't think of her as a witch at all. And even her own people told that years ago she used to come down to the valley with her herb medicines, healing people. So she couldn't be a bad person. Could she?

Callifree shivered again. It wasn't too late to turn around and go back home. But she had come this far -- and she just had to do SOMETHING about this war, before they were all killed off.

She slithered back into the cover of the forest and plodded on upward, clawing her way through the brush.

She was almost upon the woman before she realized it, and ducked behind a rock, looking at her. She wasn't so old, maybe as old as Auntie Timten, but thin and wiry. She was pounding some leaves against the rocks.

"I won't hurt you," she called out softly, and Callifree blushed. She must have been making plenty of noise as she climbed, for all she was trying not to.

She hesitated a moment, and then walked up to the woman and sat down crosslegged on the ground.

"Do you know me as Bethaa the Wise, or the Witch of West Mountain?" she said with a smile, her dark eyes glancing at Callifree keenly.

"Uh -- the witch..."

"Ah, a valley child. You're brave to come! How can I help you?"

Callifree stared at her. How indeed? She hadn't thought that far ahead. She only knew that she had talked with her uncle, and Auntie Timten, and several other people in the village about stopping this war, and had gotten nowhere. She sighed, and stared curiously at the woman.

Callifree sighed again. "You know our village has been at war with the hill village for
many years. I keep asking the elders when it's
going to stop, when we can sleep peacefully in our
beds again, when we can have enough food instead
of having it destroyed, when the killing of all
our people is going to stop. But no-one answers
me. My cousin said I spoke like you. So I have
come."

The woman continued to pound the leaves without speaking. Little sparks flew as the rocks
connected, and the green leaves turned to white
powder as she worked. With deft hands she scooped
the powder into a bag and laid out some more
leaves.

"Have you ever had enemies that are now your
friends?" Bethaa said at last.

"You mean like my older sister, Corli? We
used to fight all the time, but now that she's
married and has a baby, we are friends. You mean
like that?"

"Yes. The best way to get rid of an enemy is
to make the enemy into a friend. Didn't you find
it so with your sister?"

"Oh, but that wouldn't work with the hill
people," Callifree said with certainty.

"Why not?"

"Well because -- because they hate us and we
hate them. That will never change."

"I'm a hill person, you know. Do you hate
me?"

"That's different. You left them, and moved
here."

Bethaa sighed. "People are people, my dear. Didn't you notice as you climbed, how close together your villages really are?"

Callifree moved restlessly. "Yes, too close! Is there some way to make them move further away? Perhaps that would stop the killing."

"Hush!" Bethaa held up a hand. "Someone's coming. You'd better go into my cave until they've gone. Quickly."

Callifree had heard nothing, but she leaped to her feet, her heart beginning to pound hard, and ran for the cave mouth.

Who would be coming here -- except someone from the hill village, her enemy!

CHAPTER TWO: Gorion
****

Callifree ducked into the cave, and then had a moment's panic as she wondered if Bethaa would give her away. But it was too late for that now. There was no other way out of the cave. She looked around swiftly, noticing how neatly it was arranged. Then she heard a boy's voice outside. She froze, her back to the wall next to the entrance, and listened.

"You are Bethaa the Wise? I am Gorion."

"Welcome to my fire, Gorion."

There was a silence, and Callifree strained to listen.

"I've come to ask you how we can end this war between my village and the valley people." Callifree swallowed a gasp.

The voice went on, "We must have a plan that will kill them all off, so that never again will we be attacked in the dawn, our food destroyed and our people killed."

Callifree put her hand over her mouth, her

eyes wide. So that was Their idea of how to stop the war!

"So much blood on your hands. Do you really want that?"

"What choice have we? They never give up! Besides, they are not civilized people, there's no way to reason with them, and no reason to spare them."

Bethaa sighed, and Callifree could see the shadow of her head shaking a slow negative. "They are people like you and I, my son. How much better it would be if you could become friends with them."

"Friends! They killed my parents and my brother Tomso, and many other relatives besides."

"So you go and kill THEIR parents and brothers, and then they come back again to do the same, and it never ends."

"That is why we must destroy them completely."

Bethaa was silent for a moment. Then she began her pounding again.

"My son, once long ago there were Shambala Warriors in these hills, who were brave enough to stand up, without weapons, against those who did battle, and prevent it. Does that not sound far braver than killing the children of the valley?"

"Since there are no Shambala Warriors now, I suppose they must have all been killed off," Gorion said sneeringly.

"They left when there was no need for them. Now, I think, it is time for them to return."

"Where can I find them?"

"Only in yourself, my son."

"That is foolishness! I am only a boy!"

"Did you not come to me for my wisdom?"

There was a long silence, punctuated by the sound of rock against rock as the woman continued to pound her leaves.

"I know I am not brave enough for that."

The pounding stopped. "It comes one step at a time. First you become grateful for the gifts of the earth."

"I AM grateful."

"For all its gifts, including the people in the valley?"

There was another silence. Then, "Go on."

"Then you must learn to feel compassion for all living things, and to know that you share the same pain and sorrow. Yes, the same," she went on as Gorion snorted. "Do you not know there are children like you in the valley whose parents have been killed by these battles?"

Callifree's eyes stung with sudden tears. She was one of those. And so was this boy. Perhaps they really should feel compassion for one another.

"And if I get that far?"

"Then you will find the courage to prevent what is wrong."

There was another long silence.

"Is that all?"

"That is all, Gorion. But it takes patience and discipline."

Callifree could see the moving shadow as the boy got to his feet in one swift move.

"This is all nonsense! The valley people will never stop the killing -- we must end them once and for all!"

Without thinking, Callifree turned and moved out into the fading sunlight. "Our people say the same thing," she said. "That's why it keeps going on, don't you see?"

The boy made a leaping turn to face her, his hand going to the knife at his belt. He crouched, glaring at her with hatred. Callifree turned pale, wishing she had stayed in the cave.

"You are one of them!" the boy growled.

"Yes, and like you, I want all this killing to stop! You say my people killed your father and mother -- well, your people killed mine. When does it end?"

"When all of you are dead!" the boy shouted, frowning fiercely.

Callifree felt anger rising in her. "You people are hopeless," she said, frowning back. "You say you want the killing to stop, but you plan to keep right on doing it. That's stupid!"

"You're even stupider, silly girl..." Gorion began, but stopped in surprise as Bethaa began to laugh.

"Children, children," she said, shaking her head with a smile. "Stop and sit down, both of you, and think about what you have just been saying."

Callifree flicked her long black hair back from her shoulder, her eyes still angry. Gorion drew a careful line in the dirt with his sandal.

"Callifree, Gorion, SIT!" Bethaa added, as

neither moved.

Callifree sat down on a rock, and Gorion, after hesitating for a moment, sat cross-legged on the ground, his hand still on his knife.

Bethaa stopped her pounding and just sat there, gazing off across the valley. The only sound was the wind in the pine trees, and a wood dove calling from the forest. The sun warmed Callifree's back, and she felt herself beginning to relax, her anger fading away. She waited for Bethaa to speak, but she said nothing. Callifree watched an ant struggling along the rock with a big crumb of bread, and felt herself relaxing still more.

And still Bethaa said nothing. Callifree twitched a little, not used to sitting still so long. She began thinking about her people, and what it was like to be afraid to go to sleep at night. She thought about the men, sleeping with their spears next to them, ready to leap up at the first sign. Once long ago, the story was told, a father had been wakened by his young son, and had leaped up and killed him before he was fully awake. There was so much sorrow in the village. In both villages, she supposed.

"It's true what Gorion says," Callifree found herself saying. "My people won't stop fighting any more than his people will. We kill each other now out of hatred -- and we've forgotten the reasons why we began to hate, it all started so long ago. If we are to stop killing, first we must stop hating."

There was another silence, and then Bethaa
spoke.

"You are not as angry as you were, I think."

Callifree shook her head, and glanced over at
Gorion. He, too, shook his head, looking sheep-
ish.

"In the silence, you see, you were able to
find again your center of peace," she said. "You
have grown up with hatred. Your parents have
been killed. It is easy to feel hatred, harder to
feel friendship. But when you have found your
center of peace, then you know what is right. And
hatred is never right."

There was another silence, and then Gorion
held out his hand toward Callifree. She hesitated, and then put her own hand in his. It was a
firm hand, with work callouses on it, a hand like
Callifree's cousin's, her uncle's, her own. Maybe
-- maybe they were alike, after all. If they
were, there was surely hope!

Bethaa was smiling at them.

"It takes practice, my children, to be able
to call up that center of peace, instead of letting everyone's talk of hatred and killing fire up
your blood. Will you practice?"

"And then shall we be able to be Shambala
Warriors?" Gorion asked. "It surely takes more
bravery to stand and face the enemy with no weapons, than it does to face them hiding behind a
shield, hiding being a spear. I would like to be
that brave, but I'm not sure I can be."

"First, your center of peace. Next, gratitude for all the world. Third, oneness with all

living things. Fourth, compassion for all people.
Is that right?" Callifree said slowly, remembering
what Bethaa had told Gorion.

Bethaa nodded. "Come to me whenever you
like," she said, "but for now you'd better go."

"I will think about what you said, Wise One.
And I will never harm you, Callifree." There was
a small sound, as of wind passing in the trees,
and Gorion's shadow was gone.

Callifree hesitated. "What about you, my
child?"

"I like your method better than his," the
girl said with a smile.

Bethaa smiled back.

"I shall try to be a Shambala, too," she
said.

Bethaa nodded. "Go now -- the sun will set
sooner than you think. Go a little to the north
and you will find a path along the brook. It will
be faster for you."

"Thank you, Wise One."

She started off, thinking about what she had
heard. The boy, Gorion, was just like all the
other boys in her village, his head full of killing. But even he was reachable. Perhaps he
wouldn't do anything about Bethaa's advice. "But
I will," Callifree thought to herself. "I will, I
will, I will," she said in her head as she found
the path and started running to the beat of the
words in her head.

Then she began singing, and a song formed of
itself in her head.

"I want to be friends with you now
I don't want to fight any more
I want to have peace with you now,
I want to grow up without war.

Shambala, Shambala
Once you came and brought us peace.
Shambala, Shambala
Rise again and make war cease."

She ran in time to the music, her feet padding softly on the grass of the path, the leaves of the trees shimmering in the sunlight as she passed. Oh, the world was beautiful, and good! And she had made a beginning. She and Gorion would become Shambalaka and stop the wars, and there would be peace again.

Callifree's Song

Syncopate

Teddy Milne

{I/we} want to be friends with you now

{I/we} don't want to fight a-ny more.

{I/we} want to have peace with you now,

{I/we} want to grow up with-out war! Sham

ba- la! Sham- ba- la! Once you came and

brought us peace. Sham-ba-la, Sham-ba-la!

Rise a-gain and make war cease!

© 1987 by Teddy Milne

CHAPTER THREE: Halred
****

Gorion sped through the forest like one of the deer, so accustomed to gliding through the trees that he made little sound. Wanting time to think, he headed up, toward the ridge above his village, where he had a favorite look-out. Lying on the hot, sunny rock, he turned it all over in his mind. Was it really possible to stop this feuding after all the blood that had been spilled? Was it possible to forgive the murder of his parents? Well, as far as that went, he was sure his parents' murderer was dead now. Perhaps that was enough. It was true, it had to stop somewhere. Only how did you get to people who were filled with hatred and revenge?

He rolled over and stared up at a hawk circling over the peak. Yes, he could feel gratitude for the earth. And gratitude for friends. And maybe be willing to be friends with someone who had been an enemy. But the elders were so bitter. Maybe it was easier for the young ones -- maybe it was up to the kids to put a stop to it.

He should have arranged to meet Callifree, he thought suddenly. They should talk, become friends, bring the other kids into the Shambala plan. There was a lot to do! And first -- Bethaa was right -- they needed to practice not getting caught up in the war fever that the Old Ones were so practiced in spreading.

Gorion lay there thinking until the sunset spread orange and gold across the west, and then he ran lightly down to his village. He was hungry.

Gorion was not one to waste time. The next day he got out his favorite plaything, a small leather bag filled with clay marbles, and walked thoughtfully down to the edge of the forest. He climbed a tree and looked searchingly for Callifree with the long dark hair, but he didn't see her. Perhaps, like the girls in his village, she had house chores to do.

The sun was already swinging toward South Mountain when a boy his age, and a small girl of about six, wandered his way picking those red berries the valley people ate. There were many bushes on this hill next to the forest, and Gorion saw that he could get closer to them if he crept along the ground.

He slithered quietly down from the tree and worked his way through the bushes.

Then, his heart thumping in his chest, he stepped out. "I bet I can hit that tree over there with a stone," he said before the other boy could get over being startled. He pointed to a

huge oak with a patch of lighter bark half-way up
it. He gave a powerful throw, and the stone
whistled through the air, but fell short. The
other boy, eyeing him suspiciously, picked up a
stone and threw it towards the tree. It also fell
short.

"I think we're too far away! Let's move up
to that birch and try again."

The little girl came over to Gorion and
looked at him seriously her thumb in her mouth.

"Istobel, come away!"

"She's no bother. Your sister?"

The boy said nothing, but threw a stone towards the oak, keeping an eye on Gorion. The
stone hit the tree at its base. Gorion took
careful aim and threw his stone, hitting the white
patch dead center.

"I can do that too." The other boy tried
again, and this time hit the white patch.

"Not bad." Gorion grinned at him. "Do you
play marbles?"

"Sure." The boy pulled out a bag very much
like Gorion's, but the marbles that tumbled out
were round white stones from the brook bed, not
clay like Gorion's.

The two boys bent over the two different sets
of marbles. "I'll play you for keepsies," the
other boy said eagerly.

"Let me see, Halred!" Istobel was tugging at
his arm. Gorion showed her his clay marbles and
she touched them admiringly. "We don't have ones
like that."

"And we don't have ones like that!"

Halred was already clearing a patch of ground and marking out a circle. They played until more than half the marbles had changed hands, while Istobel watched, crowing with delight.

"Funny, isn't it. Your sister isn't the least bit afraid of me," Gorion mused.

"Too young to know any better, I suppose. Not that I'M afraid," Halred went on hurriedly.

Gorion grinned at him. "I wish we'd stop fighting while there's still some of us left alive," he said.

"Uh... me too," Halred said. "Maybe you and I could be friends, anyway."

"Okay. I'll come again sometime."

"Yeah. Okay." Gorion held out his hand and they shook solemnly. Istobel wanted to shake hands, too, so Gorion leaned over. Just then there was a tiny scream, more like a mewing, and the three of them looked up quickly.

It was Callifree. "Halred!" she said, and then, seeing it was Gorion, she sagged with relief. "Oh, it's you, Gorion."

It was Halred's turn to look startled. "You KNOW him?" he asked her in amazement.

Callifree grinned. "We were both at Bethaa's yesterday!"

"What are you talking about?" Halred said roughly. "Who's Bethaa?"

"Can't you guess? The Witch of West Mountain. Torko said I was too scared to go, so I went. She's nice. I like her."

"I guess it was pretty brave of you to go,"

Gorion said. "I'm even a little scared of her myself, and she's one of us."

"So what did she say?" Halred was holding so tight to Istobel's hand that she was almost in tears, and trying to pull away.

"She talked about the Shambala Warriors of the old days, who used to go and face the warriors, without weapons, in order to stop the fighting. And she said if we learned to really appreciate the earth and everyone in it, and feel compassion, that maybe we could stop the fighting, too." Callifree looked squarely at Gorion. "Are we really going to do it?"

Halred looked from one to the other in amazement. "We're just kids!"

"Maybe kids know better what's right than grownups do, sometimes," Gorion said. "At least we could start with us three."

"Me too, me too," said Istobel.

"Okay, we four. The four of us, at least, could decide not to fight any more."

"Sounds good to me." Callifree held out her hand to Gorion, and he took it. Halred hesitated only a moment before he added his hand to theirs, and helped Istobel put her pudgy little hand on top.

"Halred! Istobel!" A distant voice was calling.

"We have to go," Halred said. "Let's play marbles again some day soon."

Gorion nodded and glided away into the forest, and Halred and Callifree took Istobel by the arms and sped with her across the meadow.

As they ran, Callifree started singing the peace song again, and soon Halred and Istobel had learned the words and were joining in.

As they came to the village, Old Miraba came to her door, frowning suspiciously. "What's that song you're singing?" she asked. "I never heard that before."

"I made it up," Callifree said.

Miraba just looked at her. "Peace, friendship, Shamabala! All fantasy!" she mumbled.

Callifree glanced at Halred, feeling put down. But Halred whispered, "It's a good song. Don't mind her."

"Me too," Istobel whispered. They laughed, and went off to the communal lunch around the fire.

CHAPTER FOUR: Bethaa
****

"Teach me about the Shambala," Halred asked that evening when the food was gone and the fire had been built high, and the golden sparks from the fire had begun to mix with the stars. They moved away from the others and Callifree told him what Bethaa had said. They practiced finding the center of peace, and looking around them at their valley, beautiful in the moonlight, feeling grateful. Even Istobel seemed able to do it.

"Can we be Shambala Warriors, too?" Halred asked.

"Why not?"

"Tell me more about the first Shambalakas," Istobel begged.

Callifree shrugged. "Bethaa only said that much. It's all I know."

"You say Bethaa is -- is all right?" Halred stared up at West Mountain. "Not really a witch? Perhaps we could go up there and learn more about the Shambalakas."

24

"Let's go tomorrow!" Callifree jumped to her feet. "I'd like to see her again."

So, next morning early, they started out toward West Mountain. They had reached the forest and started their climb when Gorion appeared.

"I saw you from the hillside," he said with a grin. "I guessed where you were heading, and decided to join you."

"Welcome, Gorion," said Halred. "Yes, we want to hear more about the old Shambalakas."

They climbed up the path beside the brook, Halred and Gorion taking turns carrying Istobel on their backs. And at last they reached the cave of Bethaa.

She was not there, but Gorion and Halred had their marbles with them, and the three older ones played while Istobel studied the insect life on the bark of a pine tree.

In a short while, Bethaa appeared. She had been gathering herbs in the forest since daybreak, and was tired, but she was glad to see the children.

Halred seemed nervous to see her, grabbing Istobel and holding her tightly.

Bethaa noticed his fear, and smiled a little sadly. She turned to Callifree. "Tell me, do you find me ugly?"

"Oh, no!" Callifree answered, knowing she spoke the truth.

"Then you are wise for your years, young one. Stupid people think I am ugly. It is only the wise who can see beyond that, to the beauty of soul that each of us has within."

"Have I beauty of soul, too?" Callifree asked.

"Of course, child. Most young ones do. But tell me why you have come."

"Tell us about the old Shambalakas," Halred said eagerly, putting down the squirming Istobel and forgetting his fears.

"Yes, you didn't say much about them before," Gorion added. "What did they do, exactly?"

Bethaa made herself comfortable on her stone chair padded with moss, and raised her head, listening to the wind.

"It was in the time of my great-great-grandfather Ulmat, which was a long time ago," she began. "In those days we hill people were friendly with the valley people, and traded our goat's milk and mountain herbs for the valley people's wheat and vegetables.

"There was a wandering tribe that crossed the hills each summer and came down into the valley to graze their goats. The valley people were beginning to use the open fields for planting, and the goats were hardly good company for the wheat. First there were discussions, and then skirmishes, and than battles.

"A wandering storyteller was in the valley just as things were getting bad, and he told us a tale of a lost paradise in the Himalayan Mountains, there on the roof of the world, named Shambala. There, he said, people were still good and beautiful, as in the Garden of Eden, and there some day when the world was all at war, the Shambala Warriors would come out from their paradise and defeat the forces of evil, without the use of violence.

"Two young men of the valley were much struck by this story, and in the dead of night they went to the camp of the tribesmen and broke their spears in two. Then they went to their own campfire and did the same thing. In the morning when the village men went to fight again, they found they had no weapons. They raged and they swore and they stamped their feet and then they went to cut more young trees to make new spears. And by the time they had weapons again, the tribesmen had gone back over the hills. They never came again."

There was a silence. Then Halred spoke.

"I bet the tribesmen were raging and swearing, too!"

"Yes, but they had the sense to end it when they had a chance," Gorion said. "Maybe that's all we need, is something that gives us an excuse to stop."

Callifree sighed. "Well, we must keep thinking. And Gorion, isn't there anyone else in your village who might want to join us Shambala Warriors?"

"I THINK so," Gorion said. "Minro and his sister Fari might -- but they're only ten and eight years old. I'm not sure I should talk to them, because they might tell their mother."

"Maybe you could tell them the story Bethaa just told us," Callifree said eagerly, "and then ask them IF there were modern Shambalas, would they join."

"But unless I tell them about now, they wouldn't do the practicing," Gorion said.

"I know," Halred put in, "tell them it's a secret club you're starting -- don't tell them yet about us being in it, too."

"That could work. But is it fair not to tell them about you?"

"You'll have already told them it's a secret club -- that's one of the secrets!" Halred grinned, and they all laughed.

"Come, let's have an exercise right now," Bethaa said. "Think about all the people who you don't even know, who do things for you."

Callifree was puzzled. "What do you mean, Bethaa? People we don't know?"

Bethaa pointed to Callifree's feet. "You are wearing leather sandals, aren't you? And you, Gorion, are wearing a woolen shirt."

"Why yes, I got them from the wagon man."

"Me, too."

"And did you never think, Callifree, that perhaps the leather for your sandals came from the hill village animals? And did you never think, Gorion, that perhaps the wool came from the valley people's sheep?"

Gorion and Callifree stared at each other, and then began to laugh. "You mean, all this time our villages have been buying from each other through the wagon man, and we never even thought about it?"

"I never thought about someone making the things I bought -- herding the sheep, shearing the wool, spinning and weaving..."

"Oh, this war between us is SO SILLY!"
Callifree stamped her foot.

Gorion looked around at them, realizing he
had come to feel friendship for them. "Yes, it is
stupid," he said. "But do we dare break the
spears of the warriors?"

"And would it do any good?" added Halred. "I
mean, the tribesmen left the valley, but the hill
and valley villages will still be right where they
are. Perhaps it would just make them more angry,
each thinking the other had done it."

"Or worse, they would catch us doing it, and
be angry at US!" Callifree shuddered.

"What must we do, Bethaa?" Halred asked.

Bethaa pursed her lips and looked up into the
sky. She always stopped to think before she
spoke, Halred thought to himself. A good idea.

Bethaa spoke at last. "I do not know the
answer. I only know that if you are ready, a
chance will come. You must be able to recognize
it, so you can take advantage of it.

"I think you have made a good beginning,
getting to know each other and becoming friends.
The more of you there are, the easier it will be
when your opportunity comes."

Gorion sighed. "I have been braver about
getting to know valley people than I have been in
approaching my own friends. But I will talk to
Minro and his sister, today. Then there will be
six of us."

"Go then, and do it," said Bethaa. "But
first, let us have a meditation to cement our
friendships."

They sat in silence for many minutes, looking out across the valley and hearing only the sound of hammering from the distant village.

Then, with a sigh, Bethaa held out her hands to them, and they joined hands in a circle.

"Shambalaka!" she said.

Callifree started singing her new song again, at first softly, and then more strongly, as the others joined in. At the end they sat another long moment in silence, and then they said goodbye to Bethaa and started back down the mountain.

CHAPTER FIVE: Corli
****

As Callifree got closer to her sister's house, she started slowing down. On the way down the mountain she and Halred and Gorion had agreed on two things -- to meet at Bethaa's in three days time, and to speak to at least one person about peace, to get the idea circulating. But now that it came to actually talking to her sister Corli, whose husband was one of the bravest of the warriors, she realized it was going to be harder than she thought.

Before, when she had asked people why they couldn't stop fighting, she had had no answers to their questions. This time, she knew, the answers she had begun to know could lead to a quarrel.

"Callifree!" It was her sister, coming from the town square. They smiled fondly at each other. "Come on in, I just got some fine onions -- I know you like my onion soup."

Callifree followed her sister into the house. It was a pleasant place, though cluttered with baby things. "Where's little Jojo?" she now

31

asked, realizing that the baby was not, as usual, on Corli's back.

"Dann has him with him in the fields today." Corli beamed. "He's such a good father! But I'm so used to having the baby on my back, I miss him. I feel too light, as if I'll fly away without him holding me down to earth."

Callifree laughed. But then she remembered her errand, and grew sober.

"What's the matter, sis? You look like your goldfish died."

"I was just thinking -- about how when Jojo is old enough, he'll go off to war with the hill village, and maybe get killed."

Corli gave a surprised snort. "That's a thousand years away. What put such a funny notion into your head? Anyway, Jojo will be a great fighter, like his daddy. He won't get killed."

"Aren't you ever afraid for Dann?"

"Of course not! Well, maybe sometimes. I used to be. But he's always come back, and he tells me not to worry, so I guess I've gotten used to it."

"But don't you ever wish we could make peace with the hill people, so the fighting would stop?"

"How would we do that? They're savages! You can't deal with people like that. It's just part of life."

Callifree sighed. "But what if they're more like us than we think? What if we really COULD get along, if we tried? Didn't we used to get along, many years ago?"

Corli looked at her doubtfully. "Them, like US? That can't be. Why, they came here and killed our parents. Have you forgotten?"

"No, I haven't forgotten. But I expect we've gone there and killed parents, too, haven't we?"

Corli turned away and started chopping the onions. "It's disloyal to talk that way, Callifree," she said sharply. "Disloyal to our parents, disloyal to Dann and the other warriors, and disloyal to the elders. Don't you think that if there was a way to have peace, the elders would take it?"

"No, I don't!" Callifree frowned. "Haven't you been at the fire when the elders were talking? They don't see anything but fighting and killing."

There was the sound of running feet and a baby giggling, and then Dann burst in, holding Jojo.

"Is lunch ready? We're hungry. Aren't we, Jojo!"

Jojo giggled again.

"Oh, hello, Callifree."

"You'd better go now, Callifree." Corli took the baby from Dann.

"Go? Why, can't you stay for lunch, Calli?"

"No, she can't," Corli said sharply.

"Hey, what's the matter here. Quarrel?"

"It's okay, I'm going." Callifree turned and stumbled out the door. I lost my temper, she was thinking to herself. I couldn't keep my center of peace, even with my sister. I guess I need more practice, all right.

Then Dann was at her elbow. "Tell me what's the matter," he said, smiling at her kindly. "I don't want troubles in my family."

Callifree took a deep breath. "I just asked her if she didn't sometimes wish we had peace, instead of fighting all the time. She told me I was disloyal to our parents, and to you and the other warriors, and to our elders."

"Well, I don't see that," Dann said kindly. "How is it disloyal to me to want the fighting to stop? I wouldn't mind if it ended! And I hate to think of Jojo growing up and having to do what I have to do."

Callifree stared at him, her mouth hanging open in surprise. "You mean, YOU'd want peace? What a strange world this is! The warrior wants peace and the wife wants war." She shook her head in amazement. "But then why do you never speak up at the meetings by the fire?"

Dann blushed. "The brave warrior doesn't want to look like a coward, I suppose. It's hard to go against your whole village."

"But suppose there are other people, like you, who want peace but say nothing? Maybe they are waiting for someone like you to speak up. And nobody would dare call YOU a coward!"

Dann looked at her seriously, and thought for a moment. "Well...perhaps I will speak some day, if the right time ever comes."

"Sometimes you have to MAKE the right time."

Dann shrugged. "We'll see. But come on back and make peace with Corli, and stay for lunch. I'll help you patch it up."

They went back, and apparently Corli was already over her anger, or else she realized Dann wanted her to welcome Callifree, because she smiled and set a place for her at table, and nothing more was said about war and peace that day.

CHAPTER SIX: Minro
****

Gorion was in the tree hut his father had made for him before he was killed. For a long while he hadn't wanted to go there, it brought back memories that were too painful. But today he had climbed up to it, remembering instead the joy he had felt when his father had first shown it to him.

Now Gorion was wondering why he had thought avoiding the tree hut was more loyal to his father than enjoying it would have been. Surely his father had WANTED him to enjoy it!

It really was a very satisfactory place. In the breeze the oak swayed a little, like a cradle rocking a baby. It was very soothing. And to be right there among the branches, yet able to lie down and sleep, if you wanted to, without having to hold on all the time -- that was wonderful, too.

A cardinal flew onto a nearby branch, and Gorion held his breath, studying him. What a beautiful bird! He had not really noticed birds much. Why, this was what being grateful was all about -- really seeing what was all around you!

Gorion looked up into the tree with new eyes, marveling at the way the leaves danced, the way the limbs curved out and upward, all in one piece with the tree trunk. And the way the cardinal flew to another branch, hardly looking where he was going, but landing as surely as if he was just taking a step on solid ground.

And then flying off through a small opening in the branches, folding his wings to get through and then giving a mighty flap to go up. Marvelous!

Gorion lay back, his arms behind his head, feeling the swaying motion of the tree and beginning to feel sleepy.

But suddenly he became alert again. There were sounds below him, and someone was climbing up the wooden steps his father had nailed to the tree.

Cautiously, he leaned over to look. It was Minro and his sister. Just the people he wanted to see. Gorion gave a low whistle, hoping not to startle the kids and make them fall. But he could picture them losing their footing if they reached the tree hut and found him there!

Minro looked up and saw him, and stopped climbing.

"Oh," he said uncertainly. "I didn't think you ever came here any more."

"I haven't for a while. Come on up."

Minro smiled happily and started climbing again, his sister right behind him.

They climbed onto the platform and sat down in the corner, their backs to the trunk.

"I hope you don't mind we've been coming here -- it's such a neat place, and it seemed a shame to let it go to waste."

"Yes. Well." Gorion wasn't sure how he felt about it. "I guess I don't mind that you used to come, but now that I'm thinking of using it again myself, I'm not sure how I feel about finding somebody else up here."

"Yeah, I guess I'd feel the same. We'll stop coming, huh, Fari?"

Fari scowled slightly, and looked down at the ground below.

"Well, I guess you don't have to stop coming, but -- maybe we can have a set of signals so if I'm up here you'll know, and if you're up here, I'll know."

Minro's face brightened. "We'd leave anytime you wanted the place," he said eagerly.

"Okay. Let's say whenever anyone comes up here, they tie a rag on that first branch down there. Then we take it away when we go."

"Okay. But maybe we'd better go now."

"Uh -- actually, there was something I was planning to talk to you about."

"Oh?"

"Remember that day last week when I asked you if you wanted to grow up and go to war, or whether you wished the fighting would stop? And you said you hoped it would stop?"

"Well, I'm only ten. Maybe I'll be braver when I'm older." Minro looked uncomfortable.

"I heard a story about some Shambala Warriors who went out, without weapons, to prevent people from fighting and stop wars. That sounds even braver to me. I mean, they still faced the enemy, but didn't have any defense, like the warriors' shields. So maybe it's a braver thing to STOP fighting than it is to keep on fighting. What do you think?"

Minro shrugged uncertainly. "What do you want me to say?"

"Do you only say what people want you to say?" Gorion said scornfully.

"Isn't that what everybody does?" It was Minro's turn to be scornful.

Gorion looked at him thoughtfully. Then he gave a short laugh. "Maybe so. Maybe everyone says they want war when they really want peace. So maybe we'll never GET peace because no one will say what they really want. But what if those who wanted peace DID speak up? Then maybe everyone else -- or at least most people -- would admit they want peace, too."

Minro looked up at the branches overhead, and sighed. "Even at my age, kids will beat you up if you think differently from them."

Gorion remembered. But he said nothing.

"Okay, sure, I'd like to see peace. I don't want to get killed before I even grow up. And I don't want Fari to have to grow up scared, like our mother is. Our father got killed when we were little, you know."

"Yes, I know."

They were silent for a while.

Then Gorion spoke. "There's a new secret club starting, called the Shambala Warriors. We want to start talking about ending the war, to give people a chance to think about it, and maybe join us. I think you'd be welcome to join, but I'm not sure you can keep a secret."

"Sure I can!"

"What about Fari?"

"She never says anything anyway."

"That's true. Can't she talk?"

"Sure, she can, she just doesn't. Except to me."

"How do I know you can keep a secret? Tell me one you've kept."

"If I did that, I'd be proving I CAN'T keep a secret, wouldn't I?"

Gorion grinned at him. "Just testing," he said. "Okay, you can be in it if you want to be."

"I'd like to be in a secret club. But what do we have to do?"

"First, if we really want to stop the fighting, then we have to stop hating the valley people. Do you hate them?"

"They killed our father."

"They killed my father AND my mother. But I can't hate people all my life. And anyway, the valley children had nothing to do with that. So I don't hate the kids."

"Oh. I guess I don't hate the kids, either."

"Do you hate the valley kids, Fari?"

"No," she whispered shyly.

"And do you want to be in the secret club?"

"Yes." She smiled and ducked her head.

"Okay. I'll let you know when the next
meeting is going to be. Sometimes it just
happens."

"Who else is in it?"

"I can't tell you yet."

"Why not?"

"It's a secret club, remember?"

"Aw, I bet it's only you, Gorion. I don't
know anybody else that talks about peace."

"It isn't just me. There's four of us."

Minro looked at him quizzically, thinking.
Then his eyes grew wide. "You mean -- VALLEY
people are in it?" he whispered.

Gorion stared at him. This kid was smarter
than he thought. "Maybe there should be," he said
finally. "Wouldn't that be a good idea? What
better way to get peace, than if we had both sides
becoming friends! Would you still be interested
if there were valley kids in it?"

"I guess so. What are they like?"

"Just like us."

"So there ARE valley kids in it!"

"You tricked me!" Gorion jumped to his feet,
setting the tree hut swaying.

"We won't tell. I'd like to see what they're
like. I'd still like to join."

Gorion sat down again. "Okay," he said,
feeling a little reluctant. He'd been outmanoe-
vered by a younger boy, and he was feeling a bit
put out.

"I'm sorry I tricked you." Minro said with a
grin. "With my family, we wouldn't survive unless

I learned to use my wits."

Gorion knew his mother hardly ever left the house, and Minro had been going out selling the cloth she made since he was seven years old. And getting a good price, too. Gorion laughed, and felt better. "I forgot I was up against a clever businessman," he said, and held out his hand.

They shook on it, and Gorion felt relieved. Minro could turn out to be a useful ally.

CHAPTER SEVEN: Miraba
****

Halred was working in the fields, Istobel "helping" by his side. From time to time he looked around him at the other workers, wondering who he could possibly talk to about ending the fighting.

The other boys his age seemed to talk about nothing but fighting. They practiced spear throwing every evening, and liked sneaking up behind people without being heard, scaring the daylights out of them.

Halred looked down at Istobel, thankful (as he wasn't always, to be honest) that she was around, as an excuse for not joining in these war games.

Torko, especially, Callifree's cousin -- he was always begging the chief to be allowed to go with the warriors to the hill village. He had the war fever worse than some of the fighters!

Perhaps the fighters were the ones to talk to. Perhaps they knew what it was really like, killing women and children, and getting wounded.

Not glorified, like the boys saw it. But which of them might be interested? They were all praised for their bravery. Maybe they were pleased at that, and proud. Maybe even if they had better sense, their pride kept them going back into battle. Maybe they would even see it as good training for being strong and brave.

Halred sighed, and Istobel looked up at him with a question in her eyes.

"Look, there's a good bunch of wheat over there, Istobel." Istobel ran off. At her age, it was easy to turn her attention somewhere else.

Old Miraba had reached the wheat first, and Halred saw Istobel talking to her. Probably claiming it's hers, Halred thought, walking over. Miraba was smiling and handing Istobel half of the wheat, and Istobel turned to him smiling as he came up.

"Thank you, Miraba," he said apologetically. "I hope she wasn't a nuisance."

"That's all right. I like to see a girl not be bashful."

Halred laughed. "I guess that's one thing no one's ever accused Istobel of!"

Miraba laughed, too, and the three of them started gathering the wheat again.

After a few moments of silence, Miraba stood again to wipe her forehead. "I've been thinking of that song you and Callifree were singing the other day. How did that go, again?"

"I thought you said it was all fantasy," Halred mumbled, not wanting to sing it.

"But a nice fantasy, I thought. It's been running through my head, but I can't quite remember how it goes. Won't you teach it to me?"

Halred felt himself resisting, but then realized that this was his chance -- here was the person he could talk to for the Shambalas!

He started singing. "I want to be friends with you now, I don't want to fight any more," and Miraba and Istobel tried it, too. From a few yards away, Callifree's voice joined in, as she came out with water for the workers.

"Shambala, Shambala, Once you came and brought us peace. Shambala, Shambala, Rise again and make war cease!"

No one was paying that much attention, so Halred took courage, and they sang it again. Maybe if it rang in enough people's heads, it would plant some seeds and bear fruit one day, he thought.

"Do you think the Shambala Warriors might rise again and bring peace?" he asked Miraba as she stopped for a drink of water from Callifree's jug.

"Hope so," she said, and Callifree and Halred glanced at each other with secret smiles.

CHAPTER EIGHT: The Rainbow
****

The third day came, and Callifree met Halred and Istobel shortly after daybreak, to go to the meeting of the Shambalas at Bethaa's.

It was raining a soft, misty rain, and although they didn't mind getting wet, the path up the mountain was more slippery and it took them longer to climb.

When they arrived at Bethaa's cave, Gorion and two other kids were already there. Bethaa was brewing up some herb tea, and the fire felt good after the cool rain.

"Here are Minro and Fari," Gorion said, glad now to see that the club was evenly divided between valley and hill. "Minro, this is Callifree, Halred, and his sister Istobel. This is the Shambala Club."

Minro's heart had been beating wildly, waiting to meet these enemy children from the valley, but Callifree with her bright smile, and Halred with a sister even younger than Fari, were far from frightening. He sighed in relief, and heard Fari imitate him, as she often did, with a small sigh of her own.

They had the tea and took turns drying off at the fire, and then Bethaa showed them an ancient dance she knew.

First they took a partner and circled each other with palms up and touching.

"You have to really look into each other's eyes, and see that person as a real human being who is equal to you in every way," Bethaa told them.

While they circled, they sang,
"I am I,
 You are you,
 But we dance as one."

Then they stopped and clapped right hands, left hands, then both hands with each other, singing,
"I free you,
 You free me,
 We are two hands that clap."

Then they circled with each other, palm to palm again, looking into each other's eyes and singing,
"You are kind and good,
 And I'm glad you are my friend.
 May we always free each other,
 May our friendship never end."

Then they swung their partners over to another person and got a new partner to do the dance with again.

By the time they had each danced with everyone, they were all dried off!

"Look, the sun is out again," Minro said, and they all went outside.

"How beautiful it is," Halred said, looking at the trees still sparkling with rain drops, sending out sparks of color.

"Look, a rainbow!" They all looked down in the valley, and saw with amazement that a bright rainbow started in the valley village and ended where the smoke rose from the hill village in the forest.

"Our people are connected," Callifree said with awe in her voice.

"So be it," said Gorion, his face shining. He smiled at Callifree, and they all joined hands, not self-consciously, but just because of the rainbow.

They stood watching as the rain cloud moved further down the valley and the rainbow gradually faded from sight.

"I like this club," Minro said enthusiastically.

"Me too," echoed Istobel.

"Shall we meet again in three days?" Gorion asked.

They all nodded. "And, same as last time, talk to one more person about peace between now and then?"

"Yes, and let's keep singing Callifree's song," Halred said. "It stays in people's heads, even when they think they want to keep fighting."

"How does it go?" Minro asked.

So the children started down the mountain, singing Callifree's song. At the edge of the

clearing they turned to wave goodbye to Bethaa.
She stood smiling after them. Her life was not as
lonely as it had been before that day when
Callifree and Gorion had come.

Perhaps, if there was peace, she might move
back to the hill village where she had been born.
If there was peace.

Bethaa's Dance

T. Milne

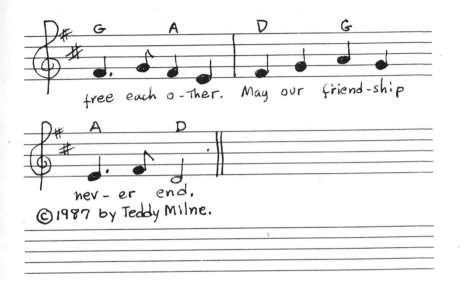

free each o-Ther. May our friend-ship

nev - er end.

© 1987 by Teddy Milne.

CHAPTER NINE: War Fever
****

The harvest was finished, but the news was
not good.   Raids from the hill people had burned
part of the crops, and with fewer people to care
for the fields after the killings, the harvest had
been poor.

"This can't go on," Maltu, the chief, was
saying that evening at the fire. "They think they
can come down here any time they want and steal
and burn and kill. We have to go up there and
teach them a lesson."

The other elders nodded, and there was a
growing grumble of war fever.

"We are becoming fewer and fewer," Maltu
said, looking around at the circle of men. "We
must start taking the younger ones with us. How
about you, Torko -- you've been begging me for
three years to go on a war party -- and you,
Halred. You are both nearly 13."

Torko beamed, but Callifree looked anxiously
at Halred, who hesitated a moment and then said,
"Istobel has only me left in the world."

Torko leaped to his feet. "I'M not a coward," he said. "I'll go!"

Ontie, one of the elders, murmured, "They're
only children, after all. Twelve years old! Has
it come to this?"

But the other elders were turning their backs
on Halred, and he started to worry. What if they
stopped letting him and Istobel eat at the common
meals? They had starved out people before now.
Biting his lip, he called out, "I'm not a coward.
I'll go, too."

Callifree looked down at the ground. "I
won't kill anyone, I swear it," he whispered to
her.

Maltu raised his arms, and there was a long
silence as the warriors prepared their minds for
battle.

Then the men around the fire began sharpening
their spears with stones. Halred joined them, his
heart in his boots. Someone handed him a spear
and he mechanically began sharpening it, as he had
done for his uncle many times before. Maltu
looked at him approvingly.

Halred glanced over at Callifree, but she was
looking down at the ground. Her hand brushed her
face, and Halred felt tears sting his own eyes.
It was time for the Shambala Warriors -- but he,
Halred, was not ready. There had not been enough
time to practice, not enough time to prepare the
mind for peace instead of war.

They should have made a plan, he realized
now. A plan to go up to the hill village in
daylight, to talk to the hill elders about peace,

to get the hill children and return to the valley
to talk to the valley elders. They might not have
killed them if they were children.

They might not have listened, either. But if
there were just one or two who began to listen --
like Ontie, perhaps.

Halred glanced over to where Callifree had
been sitting, but she had gone.

Halred looked up at the mountains, thinking
hard. What if he went and warned Gorion?

No, that would just mean that more of his own
valley people would get killed. What could he do?

But no answer came to him.

Then the sound of Callifree singing her song
of peace floated across the night. It came
closer, and the men stopped sharpening their
spears in order to listen. The song came to the
edge of the light cast by the fire, and Callifree
stood there, holding Istobel by the hand.

She spoke to the chief.

"You would take boys to kill and be killed.
What kind of men are you, to let your own sons be
killed? I tell you, this has to stop!"

She looked around the circle. Most of the
men stared at her, stony-faced. Ontie and one or
two others looked at the ground. But Miraba nodded her head, and Dann gave her an encouraging
look. Were some of the others looking uncertain?

Istobel tugged at her hand. "Tell them," she
said. Callifree looked down at her and then
straightened her back.

"Istobel and I are going up to the hill
village and ask for an end to the fighting."

"Don't speak such foolishness."

"We are! Will anyone be brave enough to go with us?"

She glared around the fire at them.

"I forbid you to go!" roared the chief. "If you tell them we're on our way to do battle with them, that will be treason, punishable by death!"

"Is death all you can think of? I challenge you to think of life! If you attack them, you are only asking for them to return and kill more of us, burn more of our crops. This must stop!"

No one spoke, and Callifree turned.

"Come on, Istobel."

Istobel trustingly took her hand again, and they left the village fire, walking toward the forest.

When they got to the edge of the woods, Callifree took a tighter grip on Istobel's hand.

"It's dark in there, Callifree."

"I know, Istobel. But Gorion will help us. Come on. Maybe we'd better sing, so they know we aren't trying to sneak up on them."

There was the sound of running, behind them, and Callifree swung around, frightened. But it was Halred.

"I told them you were right, and that I was going with you," he said, taking Istobel's other hand. "Come on."

Callifree began the song once more, "We want to be friends with you now, we don't want to fight any more," and her singing got stronger and stronger as they climbed. Halred and Istobel sang too. "We want to have peace with you now, we want to grow up without war."

Suddenly she saw the gleam of a torch among the trees, and they stopped, still singing. Gorion appeared, and Callifree almost sobbed with relief.

"Oh, Gorion, we're glad to see you! We must stop the fighting now, before my people begin a new round of killing."

Gorion gazed at her. "Your people have the war fever? So have mine! I was on the way to speak to your council of elders."

Minro and Fari stepped out of the trees. "We're going, too."

"So we're all here! Maybe we can really do it!" Callifree straightened her back. "Come on! We're nearly at your village, aren't we?"

They started up the path, and were stopped again, by a group of silent warriors with spears.

Callifree put her arms around Istobel. Gorion spread his arms as if to protect them.

"Uncle, these are my friends," he said. There was a silence. Then his uncle lifted his hand.

"You call these valley children friends? Where is your honor to your dead mother and father? How can you be friends with the killers of your family?"

"Their families were killed by our people, too. Why are they friends with ME?"

Gorion took a deep breath and looked around at his people. "I will tell you why. Because it is war, and hatred, that are our enemies, not each other."

His uncle, Barkeld the chief, made no reply.

"Uncle, did you hear the words of the song they were singing?" His voice rang out, echoing back from the rocks, as he took up the song. "We want to be friends with you now, we don't want to fight any more..."

Callifree and the others joined in, too.

"How can you come to us asking for peace, when the blood of our people has been spilled?" Barkeld asked bitterly.

"Our blood has also been spilled," Callifree said. This time, she noticed she was not speaking out of anger. When she had left the fire the first time, she had stood in the dark, looking up to the West Mountain, and finding her center of peace. Now she felt calm and strong.

"Both sides always lose!" she went on. "After what battle are you going to be ready to stop? Isn't suicide considered wrong, and even insane, in your village as it is in ours? If we stopped fighting, we would have enough crops to feed both villages, food enough for everyone. And all the children could be free to grow up without fear, to grow up as friends."

She stopped and looked around. Gorion took up the plea.

"It is time to stop, Uncle. For many years you Old Ones have talked about how to end this bloody feud. Well, now is your chance. We children have made it possible. Will you keep hatred in your hearts, and go on killing until all of us are dead? Or will you choose to see that the valley people, too, have suffered enough? Let's end the fighting, now, tonight, before there is another slaughter that will be hard to forgive!"

There was a silence. Gorion continued to stand as straight and tall as he could, but he could feel his strength ebbing away. He had done all he could do, and so had Califree. But it hadn't been enough.

Then Minro stepped forward. He went up to one of his many cousins and spoke softly, so that the other men had to strain to hear.

"Cousin, you know what war has done to our family. Yet I tell you now is the time. We must stop this war. Throw down your spear. Someone must begin. You begin."

Minro's words were almost hypnotic. His cousin gazed at him for a moment, and then threw down his spear.

Minro went to a second man. "Cousin, you have reason to kill. But you also have reason to live! Think of your newborn baby son, and help stop this fighting now. Throw down your spear."

The second man also threw down his spear.

Gorion could feel the goosebumps on his arms. Would Minro be able to do it? He was choosing his men carefully, Gorion could see, and choosing words to fit each one. Oh, he was a clever one, all right. A third man was throwing down his spear, and the fourth man threw down his before Minro even opened his mouth. This man also turned and began speaking to friends in the crowd.

Before long there was a pile of spears between Gorion and his uncle, although there were
also still many who stood belligerently, holding
their spears upright.

Gorion looked at his uncle again, across the
spears.   Then Minro was in front of his chief.
What a nerve the boy had!

"Will you be the last to throw down your
spear, oh chief?" he said challengingly.

Gorion's uncle raised his arms, and everyone
stood silently for a long, long moment.   It was
like the silence when the warriors prepared their
minds for battle, only this time it felt different.   Callifree closed her eyes and squeezed Istobel's hand so hard, Istobel tried to pull away.

Finally the chief spoke.   "Our children speak
the truth.   In our hearts we are weary of battle,
worn down by hunger and hatred.   Now we have been
given an opportunity by our children to change our
hearts and minds, and see our cousins in the
valley as people like ourselves, also weary of
battle.

"Yes, we still have feelings of sorrow, revenge and hatred, for is it not right to grieve
for those who have been killed? But if we can see
that our cousins also have feelings of revenge,
grief, and hatred, for the killing we, too, have
done, then we must feel compassion for them.

"We must take this opportunity, before our
village disappears from this beautiful earth.
Such a chance does not come to us often. We must
seize it now.

"Hear me, my people! We will go back and put away our spears, and gather up gifts of grapes and goats' milk, and go to make peace with our foes, who in ancient times were once our friends. We will become friends again. From this moment we will stop this crazy fighting that never ends."

One of the younger warriors stepped forward angrily. "What makes you think THEY will stop!"

Barkeld simply put out his hand and touched Callifree's head. The warrior looked around him, saw no one else raising his spear in anger, and shuffled back.

At first there was a silence, but then one voice, and then another, echoed Barkeld's words, "We will make peace." They ran back to the village to gather up gifts, and then started down the hill.

"Teach us your song, girl," Barkeld said roughly, and Callifree began singing again, "We want to be friends with you now, we don't want to fight any more. We want to have peace with you now, we want to grow up without war," as they marched slowly and proudly down the mountain.

The sun began to rise behind East Mountain, and daylight spread across the valley. And as they emerged from the forest onto the valley floor, the strange procession stopped and stared in amazement.

For there, coming towards them, were the valley folk, their spears gone, their arms filled with gifts of bread and vegetables. And they, too, were singing Callifree's song.

The song faltered, and then strengthened as the two groups moved toward each other, tears running down every face, to finally embrace in the wheatfields.

-o-

CHAPTER TEN: KATA ONE
****

A "Shambalaka" is a Shambala Warrior. Although we use the word "warrior," a Shambalaka is a **nonviolent** fighter for peace and justice.

A "kata" is a course you take in learning to become a Shambalaka.

As in karate and other disciplines, you are entitled to wear a different colored belt for each stage in your learning.

Karate and other eastern forms of defense, as you may know, are not exactly nonviolent. But as the old TV series, "Kung Fu," often emphasized, chops and kicks are only to be used as a last resort; FIRST you try talking, meditation, mediation, friendship. The true practicer of karate learns self-discipline, inner strength, and compassion, and aims first for nonviolent means of settling disputes.

In the Shambala kata, as with karate, to start with you wear a white belt. Instructions on how to make your own belts is in Appendix A at the back of the book.

Each kata has several parts to it. You should go through the entire kata, with all its parts, twelve times in order to complete your goal and go on to the next kata. If you are more than 12 years old, you should do the kata as many times as you are years old (up to 20).

The kata should be done at least once a week, but no more than three times a week.

KATA ONE:

1. Exercise is always a part of your training.
   Exercise (a) helps you keep fit;
              (b) is good for self-discipline, and
              (c) helps your mind to think straight.
   You may feel as if you already get enough exercise, running around, and maybe doing sports at school. But for this first kata, you need to do the exercising alone, by yourself, in order to learn mind relaxation and concentration.

   You should do the exercising for at least 20 minutes each time (unless you can't for health reasons). You can do any of these things: walk fast, jog, run, jump rope, bicycle, do fitness exercises, or you can dance to music (any kind of dancing is okay, however you want to move to the music, so long as it is exercise).

   WHILE YOU ARE EXERCISING, gradually relax your mind so that you aren't uptight about anything. You are only exercising, your whole

self, not worrying about any problems.

   After a while, before you are finished exercising, some thoughts may come bubbling up to the surface of your mind. Remember them, and write them down in your book later. To start with, these thoughts may be negative ones, especially if you've been avoiding thinking about them. As you work through the course, your thoughts should become more positive, so don't get discouraged or depressed about negative thoughts to begin with. Why get depressed about them if you know they are normal at this stage? Expect your outlook to improve as you continue with the course.

As you complete each section, write down the date and the type of exercise you did. Later, you may see that certain kinds of exercises were more helpful than others, so you will know which are best for you. Also write down any thoughts you may have had during the exercise period.

	DATE	TYPE OF EXERCISE	THOUGHTS
1.			
2.			
3.			
4.			
5.			
6.			
7.			
8.			

9.

10.

11.

12.

2. When you have finished exercising, sit down comfortably, outdoors if you can, or at a window facing outdoors if it's cold or wet. Even in the city, try to be looking at something of **nature**. Look for something you have not really noticed before or haven't thought about. It could be a flower, a blade of grass, an insect, a bird, clouds, blue sky, a tree...

Become REALLY AWARE of that thing. Think about how you are both part of the same universe, the same life force. Feel close to it. Feel liking for it. Feel it is a friend. "Commune" with it (feel "one" with it.)

Each time you go through your kata, pick a different thing.

This section could take ten minutes or an hour. Try not to let ALL your "communions" be only ten minutes. Experiment to see if a longer period of time deepens your communion or just makes you restless. You will begin to realize how long is about right for you.

When you are ready to go on to the next section, write down the date, how many minutes you spent on this section, what you found to commune with, and what you liked about it.

DATE/# MINUTES/OBJECT/WHAT YOU LIKED ABOUT IT
1.

2.

3.

4.

5.

6.

7.

8.

9.

10.

11.

12.

3. Now you can expand on your meditation. The key to this kata is **gratitude**. Think of the things you are grateful for; it can start with the object you have been meditating on, communing with. But you can also go on from there and feel gratitude for many other things -- the whole universe, perhaps, or the parts of it you like the most; your family and friends; something that's beautiful; your pet; the sunshine; the snow. Fill yourself up with gratitude. Does it feel a lot like love? Fill yourself up with love, too! Expand your list each time.

After you have meditated for a length of time that seems right, write down the things you feel grateful for. Each time just add any NEW things you feel grateful for. If at any time you don't have room in this book, start a notebook.

DATE/THINGS I AM GRATEFUL FOR
1.

2.

3.

4.

5.

6.

7.

8.

9.

10.

11.

12.

4. GIVING: Now comes the time to think
about giving something in return for all the
things you feel grateful about. Try to think of
some way to do that. You may want to plant a seed
(in an indoor pot, or outdoors) as a way of
contributing to nature. You may want to find or
make (never buy) some simple gift to give to
someone you love or care about. It could be a
picture you draw, or a poem you write, or just a
card that says "I love you." It could be a pine
cone, or seashell, or pretty stone.

Make this a different project each time, and
for a different person (or nature, or whatever).
As you approach your 12th time, think of giving
something to someone you DON'T really like very
well, but who you realize is part of your same
universe.

AT ONE-NESS: As you give your gift, to nature or to a person or whatever, try to feel "at
one" with that person, in communion; recognize the
things in you both that tie you together. Feel
the current of life and love that flows between
you. (There may be times when you will be feeling
this way and you won't get the same response from
the other person. Perhaps they are too busy, or
trying to figure out a problem, or something.
That doesn't matter. How YOU feel is what is
going to be important to you, not how THEY feel.
They may feel at-one with you some times when
YOU'RE too busy to notice, too! It all evens out
in the end.)

DATE/GIFT/RECEIVER

1.

2.

3.

4.

5.

6.

7.

8.

9.

10.

11.

12.

5. STRETCH: You want to stretch yourself beyond your home and family, and think about what gift you can give to the world for peace, or to make it a happier place where people won't feel the need for war any more. Perhaps you can write a postcard or letter to a pen pal in another city or another country; or to someone in our national government. Or you could make a phone call to the White House desk. You could say something about the things you are grateful for, and why you want peace in the world. Or perhaps you could make a peace poster and put it up in a public place.

Then make a record of it. You'll find that keeping a record helps you to think of new things to do, or to remember what gave you particular pleasure or satisfaction. Not everyone will like to do the same things. That's okay. Do what YOU like to do -- but try to make it something worth while, something life-giving, planet-saving, compassionate.

DATE/PROJECT

1.

2.

3.

4.

5.

6.

7.

8.

9.

10.

11.

12.

When you have finished doing this kata 12 (or more) times, you can make yourself a green belt to wear -- green for the beauty of the natural world, for living, growing things.

But don't skip ahead -- you will only be cheating yourself. YOU have set out to do this course. Make it mean something to you. Let it help you to be a person of honesty, integrity, character, and compassion.

Only such people can prevent wars. Through honesty, we do not close our eyes to the problems of the world; through integrity, we do not lose our determination to change things for the better; through character, we inspire others to join us in the nonviolent struggle for peace; through compassion, we remove the seeds of war by being willing to share our wealth with the poor, and our power with the powerless.

CHAPTER ELEVEN: KATA TWO
****

In Kata One, you have learned to become more
aware, to feel more gratitude for life and friends
and family, to feel at-one with nature, and to
contribute something back to life.

Always feel free to continue the exercises in
Kata One, even though you have graduated to the
next level. And when you are in level Three, you
can keep on doing the exercises in levels One and
Two, and so on. Once this book is filled up,
start a notebook to keep a record. It's good
discipline to write it down, and makes it easier
to discover the things that work best for you.

In Kata Two, you need to find other people to
do your course with. They don't have to be taking
the course, too, but you could do most of Kata One
all by yourself. Now you will need to be in
contact with others.

Wars happen because some people are greedy
and others feel unfairly treated. Wars happen
because people don't trust each other. Wars
happen because we judge other people and decide we

don't like them. Injustice, intolerance, exclusiveness, lack of trust, greed, are things we need to guard against.

KATA TWO:

As in all Katas, go through each section of Kata Two before starting the second round. Do a round at least once a week, but not more than three times a week.

1. It's best to start out with a short exercise to warm up. In Kata Two, find someone with whom you can do something cooperative, like jogging together, playing follow the leader, doing tai chi exercises, playing elbow tag, break dancing, or whatever.
   Many sports become competitive. Learn to know it when you are beginning to feel competitive. Do you like to win? Of course you do. Do you like to lose? Probably not! But if you win, doesn't that mean someone else has to lose, and feel bad? In this Kata, make it a goal to have some fun and exercise without anyone ending up feeling like a loser.
   Write down what you do, and add any thoughts about it that you might have, such as whether you liked the exercise or not, whether it got competitive, whether you were able to turn it back to a cooperative play.

DATE/EXERCISE/WITH WHOM?/THOUGHTS

1.

2.

3.

4.

5.

6.

7.

8.

9.

10.

11.

12.

2. INTERVIEWS. This could be with someone
you were just playing with, or someone else. But
half of the people you interview should be people
you don't know very well. The other half could be
people you know and like. The object is to get to
know people on a deeper level -- and sometimes
people you think you know can surprise you!

You want to ask them a question that cannot
be answered by yes or no, and has to be answered
with their own experience, not by an opinion which
they might have got from someone else. Here are
some sample questions, or you could modify these
or make up your own. But if you do make up your
own, remember the first sentence in this para-
graph!

You may want to tell people you're doing
interviews for a special project -- sometimes they
will take the question more seriously then. Or
you might prefer just to ask them in a natural
way. You could ask each person just one question,
or several. Some questions have two versions: one
if you're asking a grown-up, one if it's a kid.

Sample questions:

1a. What kind of person do you want to be
when you grow up? And what kind of person do you
want to marry?

1b. When you were a kid, what kind of person
did you want to be when you grew up? Did you
become that kind of person? What kind of person
did you want to marry? Was that kind of person
easy to find, or hard?

2. When you're angry, what sort of things do you do to get over being angry? How well do they work?

3. Tell me about the nicest person you've ever known. (If they don't say much, keep asking what they were like.)

4a. What sort of relationship do you have with each member of your family? What relationships do they have with each other? Are you satisfied with the way things are, or not? Is there anything you'd like to change?

4b. When you were growing up, what sort of relationship did you have with each member of your family? What relationships did they have with each other? Were you satisfied with the way things were? In your adult family, are relationships about the same as those earlier ones, or different? How are they different?

5. What sort of things make you appreciate nature? Can you remember a time when nature made you feel especially happy? Tell me about it.

6. What are the most important things in life, for you?

7. If you could have a perfect day, what sort of things would you do in that day?

8. Can you think of something that you are grateful for now, that you didn't really think of

being grateful for at the time?   Were you ever able to show your gratitude?

   9.   Do you know of any examples of a good deed that brought about a good result a long, long time later?   Did the person who did the good deed ever find out about it?

DATE/TALKED WITH/CONVERSATION

1.

2.

3.

4.

5.

6.

7.

8.

9.

10.

11.

12.

3. Think about someone who has done something nice for you. This exercise may be easy to start with, as you start with parents and relatives, but it may get harder as you go on down the list toward #12. But there are amazing numbers of people who contribute to your life, without you ever thinking about it. How about the farmers, who grow your food? The inventors who invented your favorite playthings? Try looking at all the things around you and realizing how many people must have been involved in producing them.

As you go through this exercise, see how connected all of us are, how dependent on each other we are. Try to feel gratitude for all the nameless people you are dependent on, and also compassion, since they may have problems and sorrows you don't know about.

Write down who you have thought of, and why you are grateful.

DATE/PERSON/REASON I'M THANKFUL

1.

2.

3.

4.

5.

6.

7.

8.

9.

10.

11.

12.

4. Now it's time to DO something that shows you are grateful to the generosity and bounty of the world. But, unlike Kata One, where you did something for the actual person, this time try to do something that will benefit us all, by "passing on" the generosity in some way.

For instance, if you are grateful for all the things your mother has done for you, "pass it on" to your little sister by doing something nice for her.

If you're grateful to the school bus driver for not getting mad when you've been extra noisy, "pass it on" by not getting mad, yourself, the next time somebody bothers you.

It may take some thinking to decide how you can "pass it on", and you also may have to wait for an opportunity -- but try to make your own opportunities to pass along good things.

And keep a record of it here, although it may be best to keep this project secret. Otherwise it's quite a temptation to brag about what you're doing, and that takes some of the benefit out of it! It's fun to do something in secret, too!

If you happen to notice any results, note them down, too -- but often results happen without our ever knowing about them. Be generous enough to let that happen without having to know! Just do your good deeds and let go of them. It's like planting a fig tree -- it doesn't bear fruit for 50 years, so I'm told, so the person who plants it has to wait a pretty long time to get anything back for his efforts -- and sometimes it's somebody else who gets the figs.

Okay: the whole point is that we want to return something to the whole planet, not just to benefit ourselves, but to benefit everybody. So if you don't have anything to put under "results," never mind!

One of your projects (or all of them!) might be to do something for peace, since that will benefit everybody. Or it could just be something that will increase the amount of love in the world, or make people more friendly. You'll have to think up your own projects for this one.

DATE/PROJECT/RESULTS?
1.

2.

3.

4.

5.

6.

7.

8.

9.

10.

11.

12.

5. You have already done some practicing with feeling "at one" with the universe. Now you should practice it with people.

If you are doing this with another person, sit on the ground or floor, close together, facing each other.

If you are alone, close your eyes and picture someone you want to know better or someone you like a lot, or someone you are having troubles with. (Try all three categories as you go through your 12).

Start with the idea that this is someone you don't know.

But you DO know something about this person -- you know that this person has felt hurt, anger, disappointment, joy, laughter, love. Because all people have felt these things. You share all things human with this person.

Picture the person as being rooted to the same roots as you are, down under the ground.

Picture yourself and the person as two drops of water in a rushing stream, rushing over the sand and rocks with millions of other drops.

Picture the common thread of your life and your humanity as something that flows through both of you and through the universe.

Picture Love as something that is part of all things in the universe, including the two of you.

But we are not trying to make ourselves love this person, we are only trying to see this other person as a PERSON LIKE YOU, not some "thing" outside of you, and nothing to do with you.

You consider yourself a PERSON. Often we see others as things -- things to use as playmates, things to pay no attention to, things to get to know and then throw away, things to love.

Let's try to see the other person not as an object, but as another person -- whole, scarred, different, weak, irritating perhaps -- but a whole person such as yourself, with a past, a present, a future -- with a RIGHT to be himself or herself, just as you have that right.

A person with a capacity to love and be generous, even if it may be hidden, as it often is in us, too!

To see this person as having an equal value to me, I may have to look at and throw out attitudes that show I'm thinking of the person as a thing. Do I want to avoid this person, or confront, or have power over, or attack? If I want those things, I'm seeing the person as a thing that is in my way.

A person is not a thing in my way, but an EQUAL whom I regard in the same way as I regard myself. We MAKE ROOM for a person. We acknowledge that person's rights, his or her capacity for goodness and love. What they want is as important as what I want. And if there is to be peace, both of us must learn to make compromises about what we want, so that we don't clash.

Perhaps you have already clashed with this person. It might help if instead of saying "that person has done such and such that I don't like," you say "things are not going the way I WANT them to go." This gives back to the other person an

equal right to have a will. It also makes us see
that the world does not necessarily have to go the
way I want it to go.

If we can really see this other person as an
equal, that's a major step toward peace. If we
are equals, we should pay as much attention to his
or her needs as we do to our own, since they have
equal value.

Whether or not you believe in God, it's helpful to believe that there is an energy, a force in
the universe toward Love, that we can tune in
with. It helps us realize our connectedness with
each other, and also shows us the way toward
reinforcing that connectedness.

We are connected whether we know it or not,
but feeling friendship, empathy, compassion for
others (Love) makes that connectedness very clear.
And the more connected we feel, the less able we
are to make war.

See if you can get to this point of feeling
equal and connected, in this exercise. You may
find that it is easier with some than with others.

At least once, do it with a real person in
front of you, and ask that person to also be doing
the exercise. Look directly into each other's
eyes, each acknowledging the other as an equal.
Welcome each other into friendship and trust.

DATE/PERSON/COMMENTS
1.

2.

3.

4.

5.

6.

7.

8.

9.

10.

11.

12.

When you have completed this kata 12 (or more) times, you may make yourself a blue belt, blue for the color of this planet as seen from space, blue for the color of our life-giving atmosphere, blue for the water that encircles the earth and gives it life.

CHAPTER TWELVE: KATA THREE
****

Kata Three concentrates on peace. First, peace within. Second, global peace. Third, family peace. Family peace is often the hardest! Because we are closer together, our wants are sometimes more often in conflict, even though we love each other.

But if family peace is hard for you, that doesn't mean that inner peace and global peace will be hard for you; they are different things.

KATA THREE

1. In Kata One you worked on "inner peace," through awareness of the world around you, gratitude, and compassion.

Now that you have also done Kata Two, you may find that the same exercise will be quite different for you.

Sit comfortably, preferably outdoors or facing nature through a window.

Think again of awareness, of gratitude, of

what you can do to repay that gratitude. Find your "center of peace" and let it grow strong and loving and full of joy. Let your body relax, piece by piece -- your toes, your feet, your legs, your fingers, your hands, your arms, your head, your neck. Wiggle each part separately and then let it go limp.

Breathe in and out slowly. Breathe in love from the loving energy of the universe. Then breathe out love to people you think of. Picture each person in the light of that love for several breaths. Do this process with at least 10 people, or for very many more than that if you have the time.

When you are finished, and get up, see how long you can maintain that inner peace and love.

DATE/COMMENTS
1.

2.

3.

4.

5.

6.

7.

8.

9.

10.

11.

12.

2. GLOBAL PEACE: Now, while you are still full of inner peace, think of ways in which you could contribute to global peace. With inner peace, nonviolence becomes natural.

Perhaps you and some friends could organize a sponsored walk for peace; or a poster contest; or a letter-writing campaign; or a petition.

Perhaps you could study some peace pamphlets until you find a fact you didn't know, and write a few letters passing on the information.

If you want to know different organizations that you could get in touch with, get a copy of "Peace Porridge One" and "Two" (see back of book).

Or try to figure out a nonviolent way to solve a problem or improve a friendship.

Taking action has two good results: it adds its weight to the already weighty demand for peace, and it helps US get over our fears for the future.

You know you are connected -- MAKE those connections, to other peace groups, other peace people. We all need each other to keep our hopes and our energy levels high. "What we can't do alone, we can do together."

DATE/PROJECT/CONNECTIONS
1.

2.

3.

4.

5.

6.

7.

8.

9.

10.

11.

12.

3. FAMILY PEACE: When my boys were 10 and 12 years old, they were quarreling all the time. It was driving me crazy. So I had a private talk with Tim, the older one, and said I'd give him $15 if he'd stop quarreling with Peter for just three weeks.

Tim was very doubtful, but he wanted the money, so he said okay. The first few days he kept coming to me saying it wasn't going to work because Peter was so rotten. But by the end of the second week, they had stopped quarreling, and never quarreled again.

They had just gotten into the HABIT of quarreling, and all they had to do was change the habit.

It's not always easy to do that, especially when it involves another person, but if Tim could do it, so can you. Don't do it for money (that was offered out of desperation.) but for Family Peace!

Of course, there are some cases where it's very hard to do, but how about trying it first before you decide it can't be done? Tim certainly thought it couldn't be done, but it happened.

If you try for three weeks and nothing changes, you don't have to keep trying if you don't want to. Nobody likes to beat their heads against a stone wall! But give it three weeks before you give up!

Your reward will be a lot more than $15.

Besides refusing to quarrel, how about trying some of the other things you've learned to do in

these katas? Things like showing appreciation,
doing secret good deeds, thinking of the other
person as an equal?

Each time you are doing your kata, think of
something new to do.

Or you may be one of those lucky people who
get along fine with everyone in your family. You
can still practice thinking of other members of
your family as equals, showing appreciation, and
so on. It may make your family relationships even
richer and stronger. And it's good practice for
having good relationships with other people, too.

122/SHAMBALA

DATE/PROJECT/COMMENTS
1.

2.

3.

4.

5.

6.

7.

8.

9.

10.

11.

12.

MAKING CONNECTIONS: Think about the things
that cause war, that have been mentioned here or
that you've heard of other places. Things like
greed, injustice, lack of trust, and intolerance.

Think of some act of greed, injustice, or
intolerance that you personally know about (maybe
it was your own act, or what someone you know did)
and make up a story in which that act leads to
war.

For instance, suppose you took most of the
cake and left only a little bit for your little
brother. Your story might be that your little
brother went out and kicked a dog. The dog bit a
neighbor. The neighbor smashed his car into
a car belonging to a man from Xyrx. That person
got so angry he told someone who owed him money
that he had to pay up right away. That man lost
all his money, and wrote a nasty article about
people from Xyrx. The government of Xyrx took a
couple of Americans hostage. Our government went
over and bombed their capital. The Xyrx's asked
for help from the Big Yuks, who had nuclear power,
and the next thing you knew, we were in a war.

Actually, there are some old folk tales along
this line, showing how one act leads to another.
Do you know any? How about "the old lady that
swallowed a fly?" or the one about the pig that
wouldn't jump over the style?

The Haudenosaunee (Iroquois Nation) have a
Great Law that "in our every deliberation we must
consider the impact of our decisions on the next
seven generations." Do you think if we did that,
we would have acid rain, toxic wastes, chemical

pollution, radioactive waste?

Maybe we should do more thinking about what we're doing before we plunge ahead with what we like to call "progress."

Look at the end of this chapter for a song about how we might have gotten our planet into trouble, "Where are you, Eden?"

And here's some space to write your stories:

DATE/STORY
1.

2.

3.

4.

5.

6.

7.

8.

9.

10.

11.

12.

Once you have passed the third kata, doing each section 12 (or more) times, you will be entitled to weave and wear a red belt. Red, the color of heroes, and of perseverance, and bravery. Red, the color of fire and of sunsets. Red, the color that many people used to call the color of war -- but which we are changing to mean the color of unity, communion, and peace.

Where are you, Eden?

T. Milne

1. I walked out one mor-ning,
2. I saw my bro-thers shiv'ring,
3. Men are ne-ver sat-is-fied.
4. With fum-bling hands I fixed my world,
5. I've used up all our rich-es,

thru the sun-shine, thru the rain. I walked out of
built a fac'try, rea-dy wear. I was glad to
smoke made crops be-gin to wi-ther. I in-vent-ed
proud of all I've done, and yet wondering why the
what will be my chil-dren's fate? Will they get back to

ALL BUT 3RD VERSE

Ed-en, and I ne-ver saw home a-gain.
help them, Ev'ry-bod-y should do his share.
pest-i-cide*
more I do, the worse things seem to get.
Eden, Or is it too late?

THIRD VERSE ONLY

(3) killed the fish-es in the ri-ver.

CHORUS!

Where are you, E-den? Must I keep

trav-'lin' on? Turned my back for just a se-cond

ALL BUT LAST TIME / LAST TIME

and you were gone. and you were gone.

OR (LAST TIME)

and you were gone. ©1987 By Teddy Milne

APPENDIX A: MAKING YOUR BELT
****

You are honor-bound to make only a belt to which you entitled. For beginning Shambala Warriors, you make a white belt.

There are two methods you could use. for both, you start by measuring your waist and add one inch for every five inches: for example, if your waist is 20 inches, you add four inches, to allow for the shortening up that happens when you weave the belt. Also add enough for tying a knot and for having the ends hang down. THEN YOU DOUBLE THAT NUMBER.

Suppose your waist is 20 inches, you add four, then add eight for the knot and ends, making 32. You double that and you end up with 64 inches.

Measure several 64-inch pieces of white yarn or white string. Four strands will give you a belt about a half inch wide; eight will make it about one inch wide.

EASY METHOD #1: Put your strands over a doorknob or the knob on a chair, or other place where you will have room to work and where you can keep the tension on the strands. Some people put the strands around their big toe, and they call Method #2 "Toe Weaving" for that reason.

Or if you like, and have one, you could pass your strands through a buckle or ring (even better is two rings) that you can use later to fasten your belt around your waist. Hang the buckle or ring from a knob or hook so you will have even tension on the strands.

You want the strands to hang down evenly on both sides (this is the reason for doubling your original number. With the strand now hanging down BOTH sides of the knob, you are actually now working with your original 32 inches). If you started out with four long strands, you now have eight strands hanging down, four on each side of the knob (or toe).

This first method is just braiding the strands together. Since you want three equal parts, it's better to have a number of strands you can divide by three; for instance, 6 or 9 (making 12 or 18 final strands).

Gather up the strands in three equal parts, and braid the belt. Your mother can probably show you how to braid if you don't know how. This method will take you a very short time. You just keep crossing the strands over each other in an even pattern.

Braiding: Start with three equal strands.

// || \\

LEFT OVER

RIGHT OVER

NEW LEFT OVER
ETC.

Keep separating the
ends so they don't
get tangled.

EASY METHOD #2: This method may take slightly longer, but can be done in an evening unless you make a mistake and have to start over!

Begin by arranging the strands as explained under Method #1.

Then, instead of braiding, you weave, like this:

1. Straighten out the strands so that you have one from the left, then one from the right, then left, etc.

2. Take the strand on the right and weave it OVER and UNDER the other strands, going from right to left. Make sure you pull it all the way through or your strands will get tangled up. The first strand is now the strand on the left, with a new strand on the right.

3. Take the new strand on the right, and weave it to the left, again starting with OVER, making sure that you are going under where the one before went over, and over where the one before went under. If you always start with OVER you should always end up with UNDER. And because you are starting each row with a different strand, it is always the same.

4. Finish off: Leave a fringe at the end. Cut the ends at the knob end, and you will have a fringe there, too. Tie a knot at each end to keep it from unraveling. Trim off the fringe so the ends are even.

You can also make belts just for fun, using different colors. A pattern will come out, and it's fun to experiment and see what different

colors will look like.   But for your Shambala
Warrior ranking, the belts are as follows:

Beginner: white belt
Passed Kata One: green belt
Passed Kata Two: blue belt
Passed Kata Three: red belt

Toe Weaving:

Keep separating
the ends, so
they don't get
tangled.

Keep tension
even.

—o—

If you are a registered member of the
LASER SHAMBALA CLUB
you are entitled to a discount of $1 from the
price of this book

SHAMBALA BADGES
(a limited supply)
are available for $2 from
PITTENBRUACH PRESS
15 Walnut Street
PO Box 553
Northampton, MA 01061

"PEACE PORRIDGE," two volumes giving hundreds of resources, groups, books, videos, summer camps, songs, etc., for kids and friends of kids. "Kids as Peacemakers"(295pp) and "Russia, to Begin With" (195pp) divide the resources between general ones and those pertaining to exchanges etc. with the USSR. The latter also contains a de-mything chapter; "Instant Russian" for those who never thought they could learn the language; and part of a book-length poem by Winifred Rawlins. Ppbk.

"WAR IS A DINOSAUR and other songs of hope, love, and weltschmerz." Contains 60 new songs by Teddy Milne plus a section on how to play piano or guitar by ear. Ppbk.

"CHOOSE LOVE," 203pp, ppbk, "Unique in the clarity of its vision, inspiring in its thoughtful, dynamic and workable alternatives for constructive social change. Recommended for anyone interested in compassionate democracy." (Leslie Brain). "Very simply, lucidly and cogently it puts forward an agenda for survival, sanity, and salvation... Splendid... absolutely right." (Adam Curle). "Thoughtful passages, lovely images, and a ton of soul" (Jan Frazier).

"ANTHONY," 197pp, ppbk, "Charming. I wasn't prepared for it to turn out to be such a powerful, attractive, and interesting book. Readers are in for a treat." (Philip Mayer). "I couldn't stop reading it...a lovely story" (Sarah Grant).

LASER, the kids' peace newsletter (monthly except July & August). Upbeat, no mushroom clouds. "Wicked good!" $12/year. Sample copy, $1.50.

"SOUL FLIGHT," a book of personal and religious poetry by Emily Powell, former pastoral counselor at Kings Chapel in Boston. "Her sources of inspiration are wide: the Old and New Testaments, nature, music. The effect is often moving." -- Maine Sunday Telegram.

"THE MATURE SPIRIT," by Philip F. Mayer, available in the fall of 1987, is a fascinating analysis of the historical Bible and the rise and fall of varying religious beliefs, leading to a naturalistic formula for attaining the "mature spirit," without which we are less than fully human. About 200 pp, ppbk. $10.95. Discount price of $8.95 is for pre-publication orders only, up to September 30, 1987.

- -

Books from PITTENBRUACH PRESS
15 Walnut St., PO Box 553
Northampton, MA 01061

TO ORDER BOOKS FROM PITTENBRUACH PRESS
15 Walnut, PO Box 553, Northampton, MA 01061

SPECIAL PRICES on books by Teddy Milne, only
    for owners of this book (no photocopies,
    please -- use this page only)

SEE DESCRIPTIONS OTHER SIDE	Reg. Price	Spec. Price
Peace Porridge One	$10.95	$9.95
Peace Porridge Two	9.95	8.95
Set of both together	19.95	17.95
Shambala Warriors	7.95	6.95
War is a Dinosaur (songs)	9.95	8.95
Choose Love	10.95	8.95
Anthony	9.95	7.95
LASER kids peace newsletter Year's subscription (10)	12.00	10.00
Also: "Soul Flight" (poems), Powell	7.95	5.95
"The Mature Spirit," Mayer	10.95	8.95

CIRCLE ITEMS WANTED. Add
   $1.25 for 1st bk, $.30 each
      add'l bk.
   Mass. residents add 5%   _____
                          TOTAL: _____

Name:_____
Address_____
City, St., Zip_____